Spanish Omelette

Story by Jackie Tidey
Illustrations by Trish Hill

NELSON PRICE MILBURN

Kel Ryan stayed with his dad for the school holidays. For the rest of the year, he lived with his mum, far away in another city.

Kel didn't see his dad very often, but when he did, they always had a good time.

"It will be fun at the beach today," said Kel, as he and his dad ate their breakfast. "I'm going to try out my new board. Can we go soon?"

"Yes. Go and get your gear. If we leave now, we'll be there before the beach gets crowded," said Dad.

Kel was in his room, getting his gear ready, when he heard the phone ring. When he went back to the kitchen, his dad said, "That was my boss at the airport. I have to go in to work this morning because they are very short of baggage handlers. People are away sick."

"Oh, no!" said Kel. "What am I going to do while you are at work?"

"I'll call Mrs Navarro from the apartment upstairs. She might be able to stay with you until I get back. Don't worry. I'll be finished by one o'clock. We can go to the beach this afternoon," said Dad.

Kel turned to the window and looked out at the lovely sunny day. He didn't want his dad to see how disappointed he was. Mrs Navarro! All she ever did was watch TV. He was going to be stuck inside the flat with her all morning, when he really wanted to be at the beach with Dad, trying out his new board in the surf.

"I'm sorry about this, Kel, but I won't be too long," said Dad, trying to cheer him up. "You could help Mrs Navarro with her English again. Last time she stayed with you, she told me afterwards what a good reader you were."

Just then there was a knock at the door and Mrs Navarro came in. Dad called "Goodbye" to Kel and was gone.

Mrs Navarro switched on the TV and sat down.

"Hello, Kel. You having good holiday?" she said in her not-very-good English.

"Hello, Mrs Navarro," said Kel. "We were going to the beach today, but now Dad's gone to work."

"He home soon," nodded Mrs Navarro.

"He **will be** home soon, Mrs Navarro," said Kel politely.

Mrs Navarro laughed. "You right, Kel. My English better, but still not good."

"Your English is much better than my Spanish," said Kel. "I can only say *goodbye* in Spanish — *adioz.*"

"*Adios*, Kel," said Mrs Navarro, politely. "*Adios.*" She began to laugh. "Not goodbye yet, Kel," she said.

"Why do you like watching the TV, Mrs Navarro, if you can't speak English very well?" asked Kel.

"I like to hear the talking," said Mrs Navarro. "I want to speak good English. Then I get job. Like in my own country. But learning English not easy."

Kel thought about what Mrs Navarro had said. It must be very hard not to know the right words.

He watched her unpacking the bags she had brought with her. She put her books for practising English on the kitchen bench. She also unpacked some potatoes and eggs and onions and olive oil.

"Kel, I have good idea. You help me with English and I teach you something Spanish. We make Spanish omelet — *tortilla Española* — for your father. How you say? Deal?"

Kel grinned and nodded his head. "It's a deal!"

Mrs Navarro turned off the TV. She sat with Kel at the table, and they went slowly through Lesson 32 in Mrs Navarro's English book. It was about using the words, **will be**.

Kel read from the book:

*'Pedro is 18. Next year he **will be** 19.'*

Then Mrs Navarro had a turn.

*'Maria is 25. Next year she **will be** 26.'*

Kel made up a sentence that wasn't in the book. "I am 8. Next year I **will be** 9."

Mrs Navarro laughed and said, "Kel is 8. Next year he **will be** 9."

Suddenly Mrs Navarro looked at her watch. "Come on, Kel. We will make *tortilla Española.* First we will wash hands!"

Kel hadn't done much cooking before this. He had never cracked open so many eggs! He looked at all the yolks in the bottom of the bowl.

"You have strong arms," said Mrs Navarro as she handed Kel the egg-beater. Kel turned the handle of the beater as fast as he could. This was fun! Mrs Navarro chopped the onions and sliced the potatoes very thinly. She was so quick at chopping and slicing, and she kept telling Kel how good he was at beating eggs.

Mrs Navarro put the onions and potatoes into the hot oil in the frying pan. When the onions and potatoes were almost cooked, she poured the eggs and salt and pepper mix over them.

"Now it cooks," she said. "We can tidy up and set the table. Your father **will be** home soon."

The omelet smelt delicious as it cooked. Kel knew his dad would like it. Soon Mrs Navarro turned the omelet onto a plate and then slipped it back into the pan to brown the other side.

She taught Kel how to say 'Spanish omelet' in Spanish — *tortilla Española.*

He practised saying it properly.

Then Kel heard a key turn in the lock.

"What's that lovely smell?" said his dad as he came in.

"Tortilla Española," said Kel and Mrs Navarro together.

"Well, it's delicious!" said Dad when they started to eat. "I've been working hard all morning and I'm hungry."

"We've been working hard, too," said Kel. "Now I know how to cook a Spanish omelet and how to say some new Spanish words."

"I think Kel deserves an afternoon at the beach. What do you think, Mrs Navarro?" said Kel's dad.

"Yes," replied Mrs Navarro. "I **will be** at home. You **will be** at the beach," she said in her very best English.

Kel grinned. "***Adios***, Mrs Navarro," he said.